Robert R. Symonds.

Copeland 1943.

THE LORD'S PRAYER

BOOKS BY ANTHONY C. DEANE

Life of Cranmer.

Time Remembered.

St Paul & his letters — he thinks his best.
    praised by C H Dodd. (p253. Time Remembered.

THE LORD'S PRAYER

BY
ANTHONY C. DEANE
CANON OF WINDSOR AND
CHAPLAIN TO H.M. THE KING

LONDON
HODDER AND STOUGHTON
PUBLISHERS

First published under the title "Our Father"
November, 1935

New Edition completely revised under the title
"The Lord's Prayer"   .   .   April, 1938

Made and Printed in Great Britain for Hodder & Stoughton, Limited,
by C. Tinling & Co., Ltd., Liverpool, London and Prescot.

Aʟ christen men ought to thinke and believe that this same praier is the most excellent and most sufficient. For neyther there is any thinge in this praier superfluous, neither there wanteth any petition, suite, or request for suche thinges as be necessarie for oure journey and passage in this worlde, or for oure furtherance to the attaininge of the lyfe and glorye everlastynge.

A Necessary Doctrine, 1543.

PREFACE

A_N earlier form of this book, under the title "Our Father," was published twelve years ago. This has been out of print for some time, but a continuing demand for a new edition has given me a welcome opportunity of re-writing many parts of the book, and of revising drastically the others. Yet the remark on p. 13 that "the New Testament of scholars is almost a different book from the New Testament of the average educated Englishman" still seems true. So far as the Lord's Prayer is concerned, these pages are an attempt to bridge the gulf. There are one or two points of detail which possibly may interest students; for instance, the interpretation of εἰς πειρασμόν suggested in Chapter VII was fortunate

enough to gain some distinguished support when it was first made in " The Expositor." But it is for the general reader that the book has been written, in the hope that it may enable him to use the Lord's Prayer with a more accurate knowledge of what its words mean.

A. C. D.

The Cloisters,
  Windsor Castle.

CONTENTS

I

INTRODUCTION

I

No other form of words has such a hold upon mankind as the few brief sentences of the Lord's Prayer. Probably never an hour passes without its use somewhere in the world. These were the first words most of us learnt by heart as little children, so that they are fragrant with memories. They are the last to be forgotten by men who have lost all else of religion. They are recited by every Christian Church, they are included in every service, from baptism to burial. They form the very heart of private devotion. People who differ on a hundred points of doctrine are linked by their common use of the Lord's Prayer. If much seems uncertain when we try, from our different points of view, to interpret the mind of the Master, at least we know beyond doubt that we do His will when we pray " Our Father . . . "

Yet because the prayer is so familiar we have the more need to guard against using it in a mechanical fashion, or with only a dim sense of its meaning. Many books have been written to examine the bearing of the Prayer upon contemporary problems of life and conduct. Exposition of that kind has been done with skill and thoroughness, so that there seems no present need to repeat it. But there is need, I think, for renewed study of another kind, which strictly should come first of all—a study less of the supposed implications of the Prayer than of the Prayer itself, a close scrutiny of its wording. If we are to use the prayer rightly, we must try to know the exact significance of its petitions. Before we can relate its teaching with ethical and social problems, we must make ourselves sure what that teaching is. We must neither rob the sentences of their full significance, nor read into them an imagined sense.

Of this the risk is greater, perhaps, than might be supposed. A large proportion of those who regularly use the Lord's Prayer have but a general sense of its meaning, and misunderstand some of its phrases. This happens partly because they have never examined the sentences in detail, being content to take them, as it were, on trust; and sometimes because they retain in later years an inaccurate interpretation given them in their school-days. An immense amount of fresh light has been thrown upon the language of the New Testament within the past few decades, and a very real need of our time is that this knowledge should be popularized, should be transferred from technical books and journals so as to become the ordinary heritage of ordinary folk. As things are now, the New Testament of scholars is almost a different book from the New Testament of the average educated Englishman.

These pages, then, are to be written with the single aim of studying the Lord's Prayer, not in its remoter applications, but in its direct and immediate significance. This is to be done by scrutinizing the actual wording of the Prayer, so that

we may place ourselves beside the disciples
to whom first it was given. Often, too,
the significance of a phrase, the intent of
its teaching, becomes clearer when we
set beside it other words spoken by the
Master on the same theme. Study of this
kind should help us to use the Prayer
with a devotion heightened by understanding.

II

We may begin by noticing that the
English version of the Paternoster which
everyone knows by heart is not taken
from the Bible but from the Prayer-book.
The word "trespass", for instance, is
not found in either the Authorised or the
Revised Version's rendering of the Lord's
Prayer. The first English Prayer-book
was issued in 1549, but there are English
versions of the Paternoster, nearly identical
with that now in use, that go back to the
13th century. Six years before the first
English Prayer-book a work was published, in the preparation of which

14

Henry VIII had a personal share, called *A Necessary Doctrine and Erudition for any Christian Man*, and in the first section of its commentary on the Paternoster it remarks that:

> it is meet and much requisite that the unlearned people should use to make their prayers in their mother tongue, which they best understand, whereby they may be the more moved and stirred unto devotion, and the more earnestly mind the thing that they pray for.

In one respect, however, the translation given in the first Prayer-book, as in all the earlier English service-books and later Prayer-books up to 1662, differs from the longer of the versions we now use. Only in 1662 was the closing doxology ("For Thine is the Kingdom," etc.) added when the Prayer occurred in a part of the service devoted to praise.*

The use of a doxology as a kind of supplement to the Prayer is an admirable custom, and goes back at least to the middle of the second century. Yet the

*The words are based on i. Chron. xxix, 11 : " Thine, O Lord, is the greatness, and the power, and the glory."

doxology did not form part of the prayer
our Lord taught, and its inclusion in
St. Matthew's Gospel (vi. 13) was due to a
mistake. When the Prayer came to be used
in public worship, some sentence of praise
was added as a conclusion. For instance,
in *The Teaching of the Twelve Apostles*,
a Greek booklet the date of which may
be as early as A.D. 130, the Prayer ends :
" For thine is the power and the glory
unto the ages." Afterwards some scribe
copying out St. Matthew's Gospel,
knowing the Prayer in its liturgical form,
would assume that the doxology must
have been left out accidentally from the
text he copied. So he would put it in,
and later scribes would copy his work
without question. In this way the
sentence beginning " For thine is the
kingdom " came to have a place in
many texts of the Matthæan Gospel,
and ultimately got into our Authorized
Version of the Bible. But it has rightly
been omitted from the Revised Version,
because the doxology is absent from all
the oldest and best MSS. of the Greek
Testament, including the Codex Sinaiticus.

Every reader will have noticed that there are two versions of the Lord's Prayer in the Gospels—one in the sixth chapter of St. Matthew, the other in the eleventh of St. Luke. They are notably different, both in wording and setting. According to St. Matthew, the Lord's Prayer was spoken as part of the Sermon on the Mount, and followed some general counsel on the right method of praying. According to St. Luke, it was given at a quite other time, in answer to a request from a disciple. We will compare the two narratives and forms of the Prayer, quoting the Revised Version, which here is more accurate than the Authorized:

St. Matthew vi. 9–13

After this manner therefore pray ye :
  Our Father which art in heaven,
  Hallowed be thy name.
  Thy kingdom come.
  Thy will be done, as in heaven, so on
    earth.
  Give us this day our daily bread.
  And forgive us our debts, as we also have
    forgiven our debtors.
  And bring us not into temptation, but
    deliver us from the evil one.

17

B

St. Luke xi. 1–4

And it came to pass, as he was praying in a certain place, that when he ceased, one of his disciples said unto him, Lord, teach us to pray, even as John also taught his disciples. And he said unto them, When ye pray, say,

Father,
Hallowed be thy name.
Thy kingdom come.
Give us day by day our daily bread.
And forgive us our sins ; for we ourselves also forgive every one that is indebted to us.
And bring us not into temptation.

The seeming discrepancies are plain. Which Gospel, then, it has been asked, records rightly the occasion of the Prayer ? Which preserves the true wording ? Did the Third Gospel abbreviate the Prayer, or the First expand it ?

Concerning the first of these questions, we may feel sure that St. Luke's narrative is true to fact, and that the Prayer was spoken, as he describes, when a disciple had asked : " Lord, teach us to pray." It seems incredible that St. Luke or his informants invented this story. It is not incredible, on the other hand, that the writer of the First Gospel, having included in the Sermon on the Mount our Lord's directions about praying, should insert immediately after them the Prayer which the Lord Himself taught. If, then, the Prayer were spoken but once by the Master, we may believe the occasion to be given rightly by St. Luke.

Of greater importance is the other question. Is the Prayer as spoken by our Lord represented more faithfully by the Matthæan version or the Lucan? The divergences between them are even greater than our English translations make plain. In Greek, I find that there are fifty-seven words in St. Matthew's version. Only twenty-five of these are used identically by St. Luke. Twenty-two words are omitted entirely by him. The remaining ten are changed to different forms.

A close study of these linguistic details lies outside the scope of this book. But the judgment of scholars has confirmed the choice made by the Church when it took the form given in St. Matthew's Gospel for daily use. The text of the

Lord's Prayer as we all have learnt and say it is, we have full right to believe, in accordance with words spoken by Jesus Christ. It has been suggested that the two evangelists must have had before them the same Greek version of the Prayer, as both include in it one word which has been found nowhere else in Greek literature. If they had, we may believe more easily that St. Luke shortened the Prayer than that St. Matthew lengthened it. Some of St. Luke's changes can be explained; once or twice, for instance, he seems, without making any substantial change of sense, to replace a word by another he himself liked and used often in his writings. As for his omissions, these too have been explained. Thus it has been supposed that he held the petition " Thy kingdom come " to imply and include " Thy will be done," so that the meaning was complete without these latter words. On the whole, then, scholars find it not difficult to account for the alterations they suppose St. Luke to have made.

On the other hand, they believe the

longer form of St. Matthew to be the more accurate. The Prayer was meant to be committed to memory, and, as an aid to this, the Rabbis (whose methods our Lord adopted) were accustomed to clothe their teaching in a symmetrical form. And the Lord's Prayer of the Matthæan version is strictly symmetrical. After the opening words of address, there are six petitions : three for God's glory, three for our needs. Of the first three, the dominant word is " Thy "—" Thy name," " Thy kingdom," " Thy will." Of the second three, the dominant word is " us " : " give us," " " forgive us," " bring us." (As we shall see later, " but deliver us " is not a separate petition.) To sum up, then : if the Prayer were delivered but once, St. Luke best describes the occasion, St. Matthew best gives us the wording of the Prayer ; and it is St. Matthew's version which we have learnt to use.

III

Yet was the Prayer taught but once? Some of the scholastic commentators seem curiously apt to take this for granted. None the less, it is an assumption which does violence both to human nature and to all we know of educational methods in our Lord's time. Through the years of His ministry He came before mankind as a Rabbi. And the method of a Rabbi was to select from his general instruction certain things which seemed of special importance, and to say these many times to his disciples, until they had them by heart, or at least were sure of their meaning. A teacher who had framed prayers for his disciples (as many Rabbis did, and as the Baptist had done for his followers) would repeat them frequently. It is for commentators who assume our Lord to have departed from this practice to show any evidence for their view. And, in fact, there is none.

Again, quite apart from the Rabbinical methods Jesus employed, is it in the least likely that He would speak His Prayer on one occasion only? St. Luke describes a moment when "a disciple"—unnamed, and presumably not of the Twelve—asked the Master for a model prayer. May we not feel sure that other disciples at other times would make the same request? And, when once our Lord had framed the Prayer, would He not, of His own accord, repeat it to different groups of people, and in the different places he visited? When two of the Gospels give different backgrounds to some part of our Lord's teaching, it is quite unnecessary to assume that one or the other must be wrong. On the contrary, when we realize how an itinerant Teacher would work, it becomes absurd to suppose that He did not repeat Himself. If He found sayings that specially went home to listeners, parables that held the attention of His audience, a form of prayer which was the best object-lesson in praying that He could give, then, as He travelled from place to place, He would use this material over and over again, sometimes varying a detail or a word to suit the special audience at the moment.

It may be taken as virtually certain that our Lord spoke His Prayer in Aramaic, and that this was the language in which habitually He conversed with the disciples. But there is reason to suppose that a large number of the Palestinian Jews, particularly in Galilee, were bi-lingual, speaking the colloquial form of Greek, which was then becoming a world-language, as well as Aramaic. It seems likely that our Lord knew Greek, for he taught in Decapolis, a Greek region, and talked with a Greek (Syro-Phœnician) woman, while it is unlikely that Pilate would have understood Aramaic. That at any time He delivered His Prayer in Greek is, on linguistic grounds, improbable. If, as may be safely assumed, the records of it in the Gospels were translations from Aramaic into Greek, we may be quite sure that special pains were taken to make the Greek version an exact rendering of the original. For the translator did not hesitate to use a most uncommon Greek word when he found that no other would precisely give the meaning of the Aramaic equivalent. And this word, as has already been mentioned, occurs in both the Matthæan and the Lucan versions.

In fact, the dilemma which asks us to choose between the two settings and versions of the Paternoster has, I believe, no real existence. No doubt the authorities are right who tell us to credit the story of St. Luke. No doubt they are right when they bid us accept the wording of the Prayer as given by St. Matthew. Yet it does not follow that the setting ascribed to the Prayer by St. Matthew is wrong, or that the version of the Prayer recorded by St. Luke was never spoken. Far more probably, I think, both Evangelists are accurate, and bring us two of the forms and two of the many times in which the Lord's Prayer was delivered.

Let us return for a moment to St. Luke's narrative. A disciple came and said, " Lord, teach us to pray." Perhaps Jesus long had wished to do that. But, as with His works of healing, He seems ever to have been constrained by a law which forbade Him to give until man had asked for the gift, had shown his sense of need. No sooner had the disciple said, "Teach us to pray," than the prayer was bestowed. There was no delay during which it was shaped into studied form. Rather, that which was spoken, and recorded by St. Luke, was, in effect, an extemporized first draft. Thus its unsymmetrical and comparatively brief form is to be understood. Later, our Lord would develop this first draft. He would expand the original wording. He would perfect the form, dividing the whole into two sections of three petitions apiece, thereby making it the more easy to remember. He would use it in His subsequent teaching. The complete and symmetrical form would be that which His followers would learn by heart and transmit to the Church. St. Luke's version would be the first extempore sketch of it, given without premeditation in reply to a question. Thus the two accounts of the two Evangelists become not contradictory, but complementary.

IV

There is one other point of seeming discrepancy, and again the true explanation may be of the same kind. St. Matthew's words are, " After this manner pray ye " ; St. Luke's, " When ye pray, say "—so that, according to the former, this Prayer is to be taken as a model for prayers of our own ; according to the latter, it is a prayer actually to be recited as it stands. But may not both accounts be true ? We may accept the Prayer both as one the wording of which is to be taken on our own lips, and one the spirit of which is to serve as a pattern when we pray, " after this fashion." Long usage of the Prayer shows us continually new stores of richness in its meaning. And the prayers we make for ourselves accord with the mind of God in proportion as their spirit and wide range and unselfishness reproduce the spirit of that pattern prayer which Jesus gave.

Thus we will turn to examine closely

the wording of that Prayer, both in order
that we may come nearer to a right
understanding of its significance, and
also because to know the Lord's Prayer
is to know how to pray.

II

THE HALLOWING OF
THE NAME

I

When we consider
the Prayer as a whole, we shall be
impressed again by its exquisite beauty
of structure. Of this many people have
never taken note. Yet it is of far more
than a merely literary interest. It confirms, I think the view that the Prayer in
its complete form—the Matthæan form
we all use—could not have been extemporized at a disciple's request, as was,
apparently, that first sketch of the Prayer
which St. Luke supplies.

Let us examine it rather more closely
before studying the individual phrases.
We have seen already that the whole is

made up of seven sentences—first, the words of address, and then two groups of three petitions each : the first three for God's glory, the second three for human needs. It seems not merely fanciful to remember that for those to whom our Lord spoke seven and three were "sacred" numbers, full of mystic meaning. Next, we may observe how each sentence of a group matches the corresponding sentence in the other group. The first petition is addressed to God as our Father, the second as our King, the third as our Master. And so in the second triplet it is to our Father that we look for sustenance, to our King for pardon, to our Master for guardianship. And again, it has been remarked that if we take the six petitions consecutively, we shall find that they begin with the glories of heaven, pass on to life on earth, and end with the powers of hell. There are further details of symmetry and parallelism which will become clear to all who will be at the pains to examine the structure with care. And, apart from their intrinsic beauty, they show us beyond doubt that the

Lord's Prayer is not, so to speak, a casual assemblage of petitions for His disciples' use, but an organic whole, thought out and contrived with transcendent skill and care. We may be sure that it did not cost our Lord nothing to achieve this work, to weld the unsymmetric sentences of the earlier form into this masterpiece. The Prayer must have greater value and significance to ourselves because it meant much to Him Who made it.

As we approach the three petitions which compose the first part, there is one other detail of arrangement to be noticed at the outset. It is not clearly to be discerned in our versions, yet it seems to have a real importance. We may feel certain, I believe, that the words " as in heaven, so on earth " (such is their order in the Greek phrase) qualify each of the three petitions making up the first part of the Prayer. They do not refer, that is, to the doing of the will alone, but equally to the hallowing of the Name and the coming of the Kingdom. Thus this first part of the Prayer is :

Our Father in heaven!
As in heaven, so on earth,
Thy name be hallowed,
Thy kingdom come,
Thy will be done.

Does not that link in a very beautiful way the three petitions, showing one great thought that runs through each? We do not merely ask, in a general and abstract way, for the hallowing of the Name, the coming of the Kingdom, and then, more precisely, for the doing of the will on earth as in heaven. Rather, the whole paragraph glows, from start to finish, with the same magnificent idealism. This springs, so to speak, from the opening words of address. We lift our hearts to God as our Father " in heaven," and the use of that term leads us to ask that, as by the angels in heaven, so here on earth by us, He may be reverenced, honoured, and obeyed.

Possibly for many of us there will be new cogency and force in the first part of the Lord's Prayer when we keep this sense in our minds.

II

Now let us look more closely at the wording and its significance.

As St. Luke records the Prayer, the opening address consists of the single word "Father." In the complete Matthæan version, we have, translating literally, "Our Father, the (Father) in the heavens." It were needless to insist upon the import of the pronoun; that is as clear as it is beautiful. It implies the doctrine of Christian brotherhood. The man who in uttermost solitude uses the Lord's Prayer must perforce pray not only for himself but for all his brethren. The man who in dejection might doubt if his weak prayers were worthy to be heard is made sure that with his own are linked the prayers of all within the brotherhood of Christ. The Creed, even when recited by a multitude, must be separate and individual; "I believe," since none may do another's believing for him; the Prayer, even when said in stark isolation, must be collective and

33

c

social, " Our Father . . . Give us . . ."
since love and unselfishness are at the
very heart of all true prayer.

It will be noticed that the Greek word
at the close of the opening phrase is
" heavens," not " heaven." Not much
stress need be laid on this, as the plural
and singular seem to be used often with
no distinction of meaning. But we may
remember the Jewish belief, echoed by
St. Paul, in a series of " heavens," so
that the grammarians may be right who
term this a " plural of majesty "—the
thought being that the Father pervades
and rules all the heavens. On the other
hand the phrase may be taken—and more
rightly, I think—as merely the equivalent
of an adjective. " Father in heaven "
and " heavenly Father " seem to be used
indifferently throughout the Gospels.
And the thought linked with the phrase
in the teaching of Christ seems to be one
not of locality but quality. His eager
desire was to show not *where* God is, but
what God is. He gave no special revelation about the setting of life in its next
stage, being content to reproduce, as in

34

the Dives and Lazarus parable, ideas
current among His audience. "Your
heavenly Father" in His speech meant
not chiefly a Father Who "dwells in
Heaven," but a Father Who is perfect.
"Heavenly," in His mind stands, then,
for "perfection," and human life on
"earth" for imperfection.

Many passages to illustrate this will
occur to the reader, as, for instance, "If
ye then, being evil, know how to give
good gifts to your children, how much
more shall your heavenly Father . . ."
Of all, however, the most significant is
the sentence in the Sermon on the Mount :
"Be ye therefore perfect, even as your
Father which is in heaven is perfect."
That command accords completely with
the opening sentence of the Paternoster.
It propounds the ideal at which, though
we cannot achieve it, we are to try to
aim. With nothing less are we to be
satisfied. And so, saying the words of
address in the Prayer, the thought they
are meant to bring is not the lifting of
our voice to One far withdrawn in
illimitable heights, but rather the thought

that we turn to Him Who is Perfect, and make His perfection the measure of our aspirations. " O Perfect Father, perfectly even here on earth, may Thy Name be hallowed, Thy Kingdom come, Thy will be done ! " That sets the key, the highest possible key, for the whole.

III

" Our Father," the Prayer begins. In Greek " Father " is the first word of the first sentence. We might wish it could have the same place in the English version, for there is no one word more characteristic of the Prayer's Maker, no word the use of which distinguishes more clearly His teaching from that of all the prophets and wise men before Him. It occurs but seven times in all the Old Testament, but there can have been scarcely a day when Jesus did not use it. During the centuries separating Old Testament from New there was very much development of religious thought ; the belief in personal immortality, the idea of a Divine Kingdom to come, were strengthened vastly within those four and a half centuries, and so prepared the way for the teaching of Christ. But the concept of God's Fatherhood was still indistinct; so far as it took shape, it viewed God's paternal relationship as existing not between Himself and individual souls, but between Himself and the Jewish nation, and its sense did not as yet go beyond an attempt to blend in one word the thoughts of God as Creator and Ruler.*

Thus we have need to remember how striking and important was that doctrine of the Fatherhood which Jesus bestowed upon the world. It was His concrete manner of insisting that God is love. The relationship He described was not merely that between Creator and created, but that pictured once for all in the parable of the Prodigal Son. There is, Jesus insisted, a spiritual kinship between God and man; we are His children, and (as St. Paul says) " because we are sons,

*This remains true, I think, when due weight has been given to all that has been urged by Dr. C. S. Montefiori in his valuable *Rabbinic Literature and Gospel Teaching* (1930) pp. 125 *et seq*.

we cry, Abba, Father." In a brief study
of the Lord's Prayer it would be out of
place to enter on a long discussion of
all that Christ's teaching of the Fatherhood implies. Yet it is necessary and
encouraging for us to remember that
when we begin His Prayer we are taught
by our Lord to address ourselves to God
not as a great invisible power, not as a
despot, not even merely as our Creator,
but as "our Father," as perfect Love,
to Whom, with the simple trustfulness
and frankness of little children, we can
tell our wants.

IV

Yet this view of God may be, indeed
sometimes has been, so over-emphasized,
so perverted out of all due proportion,
as to become misleading and dangerous.
Then the idea of the Fatherhood is
degraded, as someone has said, to a kind
of magnified Eli, and the thought of God's
illimitable righteousness and majesty is
sentimentalized away. The Lord's Prayer
is phrased as if Jesus were mindful of
this danger. The opening word brings

us to the Father, fills us with this new
revelation of His tender love for each of
His children. Yet our Lord, while giving
this, would not weaken that tremendous
sense of awe in approaching Him which
had possessed the Jews through long
generations. Because God was hence-
forth to be known as the Father, more,
and not less than before, must the thought
of Him fill man with humblest reverence.
So we see again the exquisite poise and
balance in the teaching of Jesus, shown
by the structure of His Prayer. When we
have been taught to invoke God as " Our
Father," immediately the first petition
that follows is that we may honour Him
profoundly on earth, even as the angels do
in heaven. First " Our Father," and then
immediately, " Hallowed be Thy name."

The meaning of this petition would
be evident to all whom Jesus taught, for
it was an accustomed beginning to Jewish
prayers. But its force is less generally
understood by people of our own time,
who often do not realize for what
" Name " stood, in Jewish usage. And
indeed its precise force is not easy to set

down in English words. But, approximately, " God's Name " means God as He discloses Himself to man. The Name is not an impersonal revelation about God, but God as He has vouchsafed to show Himself. And so the prayer is that He may be worshipped and held in profoundest awe, that the Truth He has revealed of Himself may be held sacred, that most humbly we on earth may do Him homage, even as do the triumphant hosts of heaven. As we use these words, we ourselves worship ; we pray that we may ever do so rightly ; and we ask that everywhere God's revelation of Himself may be received and reverenced. We echo the cry of *Magnificat*, " and holy is his name," and our prayer is akin to that which the Fourth Gospel attributes to our Lord Himself : " Father, glorify thy name."

So the meaning of the first petition becomes clear, and the need that we should make it is greater than it was for the disciples who first heard the Prayer. In our age the danger is more considerable of losing that sense of awe with which we should approach God. The sentence has a special significance for us in regard to our study of the Bible and theological discussions. It is good for us to examine God's revelation, to ponder the union of human and divine in the Person and words of our Lord, to bring all modern knowledge—which is, indeed, a part of God's revelation—to assist us in our search for truth. Yet we shall miss our way unless we undertake such studies in the right spirit, losing nothing of the infinite awe with which the saints of old touched holy things.

In ordinary life and speech, again, we need to pray for a deeper sense of reverence. God reveals Himself in many ways—through the Christ Who " declared His Name," through nature, through experience. We need to treat all this revelation as deeply sacred, and be resolved that it shall not have a lessened value through us for those who come after. Through our example, we ask, through our lives, through our spirit of lowly awe, Hallowed be Thy Name !

III

THE KINGDOM

I

AN early sentence of the earliest Evangelist states that " Jesus came preaching the gospel of the kingdom of God." The phrase might be used to epitomize almost all His public ministry. The Kingdom was His dominant theme. By deed and by example, no less than by word, He toiled to expound it. We can hardly turn a page of the Gospels without finding some reference to " the Kingdom of God "—or its equivalent, in St. Matthew, " the Kingdom of Heaven." It is the central *motif* of our Lord's teaching. The Kingdom is to be sought before all else. No sacrifice is too great which makes entrance to it less difficult. The laws and conditions of finding place within it are laid down, and even to be not far from it is high encouragement.

With indefatigable labour the Master tries to make plain this doctrine of the Kingdom. "Unto what shall we liken it?" He asks, and replies with a succession of swift and vivid pictures which may help His hearers to understand. It is like a grain of mustard-seed, like leaven, like a net, like a man sowing, like a pearl of great price, like a treasure in comparison with which all others are nothing worth.

Because the Kingdom has this prominent place in the doctrine of Jesus, it has been studied eagerly in each age of the Church, and interpreted from many points of view. Perhaps the chief advance in our own time towards understanding it rightly has been in discerning its comprehensiveness. Many of the past interpreters were right when they claimed that their statement of the doctrine accorded with words spoken by Christ, but wrong in supposing this one line of interpretation to be sufficient, and all others needless or mistaken. It was a very wide, as well as a very deep, idea that our Lord set before mankind when

43

He preached the Gospel of the Kingdom. Plainly, anything like a full study of the teaching about the Kingdom of God could not be attempted here. It has formed the theme of many volumes, and will form the theme, doubtless, of many more. On the other hand, we are bound to arrive, if we can, at the central idea of the phrase as our Lord employed it, for we cannot use the Lord's Prayer well until we know what it is we ask when we pray " Thy kingdom come." We must wish to find not so much a meaning for the words which satisfies modern conceptions as the meaning they had for our Lord, and the reason why He instructed His disciples to use them in the supreme Prayer.

II

Through a long period of national misfortune the Jews had consoled themselves by looking forward to a coming of the Kingdom of God. This hope might seem to make easier the task of

Christ, since to speak of the Kingdom
was to use a word familiar already, and
to name that which the coming Messiah
was expected to establish. Yet it was a
hindrance too, because, while " the Kingdom of God " was an accustomed phrase,
the meaning in which our Lord used it
was altogether new. It had been the
theme of Apocalyptic through about two
centuries before Christ came, and these
writings had made the people look forward to a sudden manifestation of Divine
power. The coming of the Kingdom
was to mean the restitution of the Jewish
people and the overthrow of alien rule.
But it had a spiritual side also—the
vindication of righteousness and the
destruction of those who had rejected
God. Some supposed that the Kingdom
would be established in this world, others
in the next. All anticipated that it would
be heralded by a sudden and catastrophic
manifestation of the Divine sovereignty.
A considerable literature fostered this
belief, and served to console Israel through
years of political subjugation and steadily
increasing economic difficulty. When

they heard John the Baptist, the people believed that the day of freedom and the advent of the national leader were at hand.

Jesus spoke, then, to people steeped in this belief—people looking anxiously for the coming of the Kingdom of God. But they expected it to be local, and national, and sudden; Jesus meant it to be world-wide, and spiritual, and of slow growth. In His view it was to be not outward but inward; to take effect not through a reformed government but through a transformed heart. It was to bring all human life into the realm of God. Its basis was to be character, and the Sermon on the Mount was a description of the kind of character for which there would be place within the Kingdom, and of the laws, the new kind of "righteousness," by which such a character must be controlled. Moreover, it was to be a kingdom having Christ Himself for its Founder and its King.

So much seems clear. Yet there remain questions to be asked concerning Christ's view of the Kingdom of God. Did it

seem to Him a present reality or a future
ideal? Was it to be an invisible union
linking together His followers, or was it
to possess a definite and visible organization? If so, was it but another name
for the Church? Again, ought its scope
to be limited to the spiritual life, or
should it have relations with the social
and political systems of each age?

We may answer, I think, that the
Kingdom of God as our Lord saw it
was both present and future. On the
one hand, He spoke of it as having come
already and being in the midst of the
disciples; on the other, He referred to
those who should see its coming with
power in the future. Here His teaching
was sometimes in close likeness to that
of Apocalyptic. But He insisted also that
the Kingdom was present already, and
would grow like a grain of mustard seed.
Thus it was both a gift to be received and
an ideal to be achieved. Again, the
Kingdom was not one with the Church,
though the task of the Church must be
to help forward its growth and to guard
what has been gained already for the

47

Kingdom. To the remaining question, perhaps our first reply must be that the supposed boundary line between, on the one hand, the "spiritual," and, the other, the political and social aspects of human life, does not properly exist, and that many of our worst blunders have their root in this false distinction. Yet, dealing with the question as it stands, we may affirm that our Lord left us in no doubt concerning the practical effect of His Kingdom upon the life of the world. It would transform that life, but it would bring to pass the changes very slowly, and working from within. There would be no sudden and dramatic upheaval, such as the Jews had expected. There would be no immediate revolution in the forms of government or in the social fabric. The Kingdom would begin by changing not institutions but men. Slowly, like leaven, its influence would spread, until the whole mass of human life was altered by its power. The method was to be not of changed institutions in the hope of bringing to pass a better life, but of a changed life which in time would

48

create better institutions. The Kingdom
of God " within you " must be the source
of the Kingdom without.

III

All this is, of course, but a summary of
truths with which by this time most of us
are well acquainted. They have been
put before us, with a large measure of
agreement, by various writers who have
set themselves to study our Lord's con-
ception of " the Kingdom of God." They
are conclusions not likely to be over-
thrown, and they have rightly displaced
mistaken theories about the Kingdom—
especially those which identified it
exclusively with the Church, and those
which, in effect, postponed the advent of
the Kingdom to " the end of the world."
Valuable, however, as they are, and true
so far as they go, I doubt if, by themselves, they are adequate. When we want
to know for what the Kingdom of God
stood in the mind of Jesus, it is natural

49

that we should concentrate our attention upon those sayings of His in which He speaks of it directly. And this is, in the main, what scholars have done, and done most admirably, in recent years. Yet a wider view is needed, to be derived not merely from special passages of our Lord's teaching, but from the whole tenor of His life, His whole outlook on the relations between God and man. When we try to take such a view we place ourselves necessarily farther from framing precise and convenient definitions, but nearer, maybe, to understanding the mind of Christ.

For surely the teaching of the Kingdom was not meant merely to propound one special scheme of human development, or one special method of divine guidance. Rather, it was an attempt to set forth a vast idea embracing all existence, in this stage of life and beyond, " as in heaven, so on earth." The idea in its fulness transcends human speech, and our Lord Himself could not find any one form of words or illustration to describe it adequately. He must be content if by reiterated teaching, by clothing now this, now another aspect of it in a parable, He might at length make partly clear to His disciples what was luminously evident to Himself.

Life, as He saw it, was not a transient physical condition ; this was, relatively, of small importance. To live was to be in right relation with God, to be permeated with the sense of His all-pervading nearness and holiness and love and power. Our Lord Himself was ever thrilled through and through with this consciousness of the Father, to do Whose will, therefore, must be the passion and glory of all true life. Let any man truly realize God, and he must love Him and his fellow-men ; this sense of God must become his overmastering and eager enthusiasm, dominating every act and thought. Then, from sheer love, God would be his King, and so, acknowledging and serving Him in joy, a man would pass from death into life, would gain place in the Kingdom of God. With Him would be linked others afire with the same enthusiasm for God, and so the Kingdom would become a visible society in this world, so its influence would spread. If only men would overcome the sin or blindness which shuts their eyes to the joy of serving God! If only they would simplify existence and gain freedom from care by making the doing of His will their one law! What happiness would be theirs, and how the world would be transformed! Already there were a few who had entered on this life, in whom something like a true consciousness of God's immanent power and love was beginning to dawn; through these, and through His own work, the Kingdom was already here. "The kingdom of God is among you!" Yet how few were within its sway, how many without! Therefore let the disciple pray "Thy kingdom come." To open that gateway of the soul that the glory of God might pour through it, to let the inward rush of power possess the life until every thought and act became its outcome, to merge human will joyously in the divine will until a single motive co-ordinated all existence—that, it seems, was the life which Jesus Himself lived, and the life He described to others under the figure of entering the Kingdom of God.

IV

At least such an explanation brings us nearer, I believe to the real meaning of the phrase as our Lord used it than the more precise and literal interpretations of the accustomed type. The Kingdom, then, is not a social organization, or an institution, or an event to come. Rather, it is an attempt to describe figuratively the one true mode of life, life begun here with a physical setting, but indestructible by what we name death. And to make that view understood more easily our Lord set it forth under the figure of the Kingdom, because for the advent of a Kingdom of God the people were looking. Yet if we find it hard to realize our Lord's standpoint and to see life as He saw it, can we wonder that His ideal baffled most of those to whom He spoke? God was for them a

Being awful and remote. Righteousness was a technical virtue, to be attained by a punctilious observance of the Rabbinic code. The whole teaching of Jesus was bewilderingly novel. "What is this! A new doctrine!" they cried in amazement. Only those who were ready to trust and to try, to experiment by leading the kind of life which the Master prescribed, found that it made all things clear, that the due love of God and neighbour were its logical outcome. Thereafter they might fail often to realize the ideal. But no longer could they doubt what the true ideal was. To lead a life hid with Christ in God was to enter the Kingdom. To strive that all men might share this overmastering consciousness of God was to pray "Thy kingdom come"—to ask and to work that God's sovereignty might be complete everywhere, in earth as in heaven.

So we return to this sentence of the Paternoster. What is it that most people have in mind when they say, "Thy Kingdom come"? With a few, retaining unconsciously the old Apocalyptic idea, it is a prayer for the speedy return of Christ as King, and the end of the world. Others use the sentence as asking only that their inner hearts may obey Christ and conquer the rival powers of evil. Yet others, influenced by the tradition which St. Augustine did much to popularize, take the Kingdom to be but another name for the Church, and find in this sentence chiefly a prayer for the Church's progress. But, as we have seen, none of these interpretations is satisfying or adequate. Our Lord's words about the end of the world are coloured so largely by, and take so much of their imagery from, the Apocalyptic writings that it seems rash to interpret them with a crude literalism. And, unmistakably, "Thy kingdom come" was meant to be a prayer for the world's trend, not for the world's end. With reiterated emphasis He made it clear that the Kingdom was to be set up in this world—was, indeed, already here when He spoke, even though its full completion must be hereafter. Of the second interpretation we need say no more than that this petition must not

be made virtually identical with that
which stands later in the Prayer, " Lead
us not into temptation, but deliver us
from evil."   And lastly, while to pray for
the work of the Church must obviously be
right, and while the growth of the Church
may be a witness to the growth of the
Kingdom, nevertheless the Kingdom is
distinct from, and wider than, the Church.
We must not narrow the spirit of the
Prayer.

V

And is not the wider meaning—in a
sense, more simple, yet more profound
—that also which satisfies best, and gives
the words their richest meaning ?   In the
soul of Jesus, we may say with all reverence, the reign of God was supreme.   He
longed, and bade us pray, that this glorious
consciousness of, and obedience to, God's
reign should be shared by all human
beings.   That, surely, is what we ask
when we pray " Thy kingdom come."

We ask it first for the glory of God,

because it is His due. Even the cadence
of the words in Greek marks this. There
is an effect of reiterated emphasis, difficult
to reproduce in English, as, immediately
after a light unaccented vowel, the heavy
monosyllable (meaning " Thine ") falls
on the ear at the close of each of the first
three petitions in the Lord's Prayer.
" Let the name that is hallowed be Thine ;
let the kingdom to come be Thine ;
let the will to be done be Thine " may
give some idea of this effect. Plainly it
is deliberate, and another illustration of
what we may dare to call the artistic
structure of the Prayer. It insists that
the common aim of all these first three
petitions is the advancement of God's
glory ; petitions for our own needs
follow in the second part of the Prayer.
Yet, mindful that we ask it primarily for
God's sake, we may make the request for
ourselves also, because there can be no
happiness like that which comes from
having God enthroned in our souls. And
we ask it for others also, both that God's
purpose may be completed, and that the
great community of lives pervaded by

the consciousness of God may increase, as Jesus desired.

For, indeed, this magnificent petition includes all prayers for our organized social life, and, in a sense, makes most of them superfluous. We pray for the growth of the Church, for a spirit of concord among Christians, for peace among nations, for an ending of rancour and strife between classes, for social righteous-ness—we can multiply such intercessions almost endlessly, and the need of them is real. But could we bring about the perfect fulfilment (" as in heaven, so on earth ") of this one thing, " Thy kingdom come," all else for which we pray would follow. When once the reign of God controlled the hearts of men, when once His realm was everything to them, as it was to our Lord, what social problem or bitterness would not be in sight of its end ? All these things would " be added" to us, if first, by prayer and deed, we sought the Kingdom of God, and set ourselves to bring nearer that which we ask for when we pray " Thy kingdom come ! "

IV

THE DOING OF THE WILL

I

ALREADY we have seen the Paternoster to be no string of unrelated petitions, brought together without premeditated design, but a symmetrical structure, framed with exquisite skill. And at this point let us pause for a moment to observe the manner in which in this part of the Prayer each sentence leads logically to the next. We begin by praying that God's revelation of Himself may be held in perfect awe and reverence. What is needed to stir that awe and reverence in the hearts of men? That they should live in a radiant sense of God, in a consciousness of His all-pervading realm and its claims; in other words, that they should be within His Kingdom. In order, therefore, that His name may be hallowed rightly, we ask that His Kingdom may come. What again, will make that coming possible? By what means shall men become sure of God, and be convinced that the doctrine of His Kingdom is true? There is only one way. They must do His will. "If any man will do his will he shall know of the doctrine, whether it be of God." "Not every one that saith unto me, Lord, Lord, shall enter into the kingdom of heaven, but he that doeth the will." It is, then, in logical sequence to praying, "Thy kingdom come" that we pray next "Thy will be done." And thus the more closely we examine the structure of the Prayer, the more, I am sure, shall we discern its beauty and revere the wisdom which contrived it.

Perhaps some of us may need to guard ourselves against a misunderstanding of all this first part of the Lord's Prayer, which is, I think, rather common. To phrase it crudely, many people say the words in the sense of expressing a pious hope that God will work out His purposes while mankind gratefully or submissively looks on. The idea of their petitions is of asking God to cause His Name to be hallowed, to establish His Kingdom and to carry out His will. But Divine power, by its own law, can do none of these things without the co-operation of human effort. These first sentences of the Pater-noster are not just so many requests that things may be done. They are prayers that, with God's help, we may do things. They ask that that we, and our fellow-men, may hallow the name, that in and by us the Kingdom may come, that by us God's will may be done. And most of all, perhaps, in relation with the last of the three petitions does this truth need to be kept in mind. When people say, " God's will be done," they mean, as a rule, that if something they dislike is to befall them, they will try to bear it patiently. Although it is not what they would have chosen, nevertheless let God accomplish His purpose. There are special circumstances, no doubt, when this may be a most right and noble prayer. But, when made generally, it is apt to give the effect of a bewildered and not quite unresentful acquiescence. Of this

an unfortunate example is supplied by
a well-known hymn. Its suggestion—
which, obviously, its writer cannot have
intended—is that God multiplies mis-
fortunes on those who love Him; the
stanzas are a kind of catalogue of calami-
ties, and on each follows the refrain,
" Thy will be done." Much might be
said of the harm wrought by such teaching.
The one point, however, which concerns
us here is that it misunderstands strangely
the petition of the Lord's Prayer, which we
are now considering. As Jesus taught
us to use them, the words " Thy will be
done " are not a prayer for passive
resignation. They are a prayer for active
service. They do not mean chiefly " May
God do His will," but "May we do God's
will." And we ask that we may do it,
not of constraint but of choice ; even as
the angels do it, not because they must,
but because they love. " As in heaven,
so on earth."

II

To be sure that we interpret rightly this, as the other sentences of the Paternoster, we must needs turn not to any author of hymns, not to any great saint whose asceticism may have tinged the Christian thought of his time, but to the words and example of Jesus Himself. These show that the supreme purpose of His life was ever to do the will of the Father. "My meat is to do the will of him that sent me." "I seek not mine own will, but the will of him that sent me." "For I am come down from heaven, not to do mine own will, but the will of him that sent me." With this repeated emphasis He insists upon the fact : "to do the will"—not merely to bear, but to do—"of him that sent me" is His own definition of His ministry. And He bids men have the same aim : that man shall be admitted to the Kingdom who "does the will of my Father"; they who strive for it are recognized as His spiritual kindred : "Whosoever shall do the will of God, the same is my brother, and my sister, and mother."

Remembering that, Christ plainly set before Himself the doing of the Father's will as His purpose, and insisted repeatedly that the active doing of the will is the test of true discipleship, we may wonder how the sentence from his Prayer came to be misunderstood, and weakened into a profession of patient submission. The answer lies, no doubt, in the wrong sense people have attached to the words spoken in the Garden of Gethsemane. "Not as I will, but as thou wilt," He cried to the Father, and used again the very phrase He had taught others to use, "Thy will be done." This has been taken popularly to mean, in effect, that He desired the Father's purpose to be worked out, while the Son bowed to it submissively. Thus the sentence has been accounted a prayer for the spirit of patience, for fortitude to bear, for uncomplaining resignation. But this is, if not a quite false, at least a quite inadequate, view. When Jesus prayed "Thy will be done," in Gethsemane,

He would not have ended the sentence " Thy will be done by Thee," but " Thy will be done by Me."

Then, with supreme resolve in that supreme hour, He bent Himself again to the task. There was but a short space left before the Crucifixion, yet there were ways still in which the Father's will might be done. And it is well for us to notice what has been termed " the animation of our Lord's surrender," the passion of His Passion. He did not merely accept what came ; up to the very end He sought eagerly for opportunities of ministering, as the Father willed, to the souls of men. Even on the Cross there were murderers to be prayed for, and a penitent to be pardoned, and a mother to be sheltered, until at last He was able—as none else ever has been able—to cry, " It is finished." All was complete. The Father's will was done.

III

Therefore the words and deeds of Jesus show quite plainly what He had

65

E

in mind when He bade His disciples use
this sentence of His Prayer. They were
to ask that they might follow the rule
of life which had been His own, and
dedicate themselves without reserve to
doing the will of God. Through men
united by that aim would the Kingdom
come. We need often, and then may
ask fitly, a submissive spirit, resignation
to bear trials the reason for which lies
beyond our understanding. Yet in the
Paternoster, that for which we ask God's
help is not that we may bear, but that we
may do; that we may have insight to
recognize our opportunities of service
and strength to use them. The thought
could not be summarized better than it
is in one of the Prayer-book collects,
which asks for God's people " that they
may both perceive and know what things
they ought to do, and also may have
grace and power faithfully to fulfil the
same."

Nothing, perhaps, so helps us to measure
the difference in scope between the
" negative " and " positive " interpretations of this petition as to ponder the

results if the prayer were perfectly fulfilled. Were that achieved when "Thy will be done" is given its common "negative" meaning, patience would be complete. There would be no murmuring against the decrees of Providence. We should bear readily whatever of strain or burden was imposed upon us by God. Ours would be that trusting spirit of submission for which our saying of the words is popularly supposed to ask. That would bring, no doubt, some real gain, provided that we did not ascribe to God sufferings actually due to our own fault or to the malignant powers of evil. At best, though, how small the gain would seem when set beside the fulfilment of "Thy will be done" in its positive sense! First, for our individual selves, this would mean that every one of us had an immensely simplified life. Every moment of it would be controlled by one law, the doing of God's will. We should care for this, and for nothing else. Thereby we should escape the tangle of rival motives, and achieve something of that serene tranquillity with which the unhurried Master

67

moved from one day to another, from one task to the next. To be singly bent on doing the will of God is to know the secret of His composure.

Or, think, again, of the result on our common life. How vastly its quarrels and acerbities would be lessened! Differences of opinion, no doubt, would remain, due as they are to diversities of temperament and education and experience. But our social problems would be faced in a new spirit. In a sense, our "unhappy divisions," ecclesiastical or political, need not be unhappy at all, but rather a sign of life. Truth will ever remain greater than any one individual's, or party's, powers of perception; each will see some aspect which is invisible to others. The existence of "divisions," then, is a sign that our beliefs are honest, that we are trying to see as much as we can of truth for ourselves. What is "unhappy" is the spirit of rancour between those honestly divided, not the divisions themselves. And rancour must vanish between those, of views however divergent, who are united by a common effort to fulfil this petition of the Lord's Prayer.

Let us take a concrete example. Suppose some great industrial dispute to be in progress. At length (it should be at the start) representatives of the two sides are brought together for conference. As things are now, probably each side is anxious for a victory, or, at best, for a settlement which keeps as much and gives as little as is necessary for some sort of workable compromise. But suppose that the representatives of the two parties met with the one desire, not to score a victory, not to patch up some kind of working compromise, but to do the will of God? Suppose that their first act was to pray together " Thy will be done," and that then they set themselves resolutely to see how they could accomplish this? It would remain for them, obviously, to decide what way God's will pointed, and often this would be interpreted at first with marked differences. But soon—incredibly soon, as the world would judge—those who had met in this spirit, had prayed together that they might do God's will, and had put aside all lower aims, would find themselves in agreement. This may seem a fantastic picture. There would be nothing impossible in it were ours in truth a Christian country, or even if all those who habitually pray "Thy will be done" felt and obeyed the real meaning of the words.

Imagine once more this same motive to control international councils, so that the question asked by each nation was not "How can we consolidate our position?" "How can we achieve security?" "How can we increase our trade?"—but, "How can we do God's will?" Again a far-off vision! Yet it is only along this road that the world will arrive at real peace, when the ideals of Christ are seen to be of practical wisdom, when this sentence of the Lord's Prayer becomes not merely the aspiration of our lips, but the one purpose of our deeds, and with an earnestness undaunted by failures, no matter how many, we set ourselves to hallow God's name, to build His Kingdom, and to do His will—on earth, even as in Heaven.

V

TO-MORROW'S BREAD

I

We have now to consider the second part of the Lord's Prayer: which teaches us, having made petitions for God's glory, to add others about our human needs. Yet these sentences too must be unselfish; whatever we ask is not for our individual selves alone, but for our fellow-men. Therefore the prayer can never be inopportune. If there be any want made known by it which is not ours at the moment, we may be sure that it is felt acutely by myriads of others, and for them we intercede. And there is great comfort in the thought that we are encouraged by Jesus to speak thus to our Father; not merely to worship or to petition for the growth of His Kingdom, but to pray about our own human wants, and to be confident that He will answer. It seems a fact of vast significance, not to be ignored in any discussion of prayer and its efficacy, that He Who knew both human nature and the mind of God beyond all other should have been explicit in His certainty about prayer and the wide scope of its power.

In considering the second part of the Paternoster let us follow the same general line as before, concerning ourselves less with remoter applications of the words than with the words themselves, and trying to elicit their exact meaning. I am sure that the need of this is greater than most of us, naturally enough, imagine.

Thus we may suppose that there can be no difficulty over the meaning of the petition which we know in the form " Give us this day our daily bread." Yet, in point of fact, no other sentence of the Paternoster has been the theme of such prolonged debate among scholars. The whole difficulty was caused by one word—the mysterious adjective *epiousios* prefixed to " bread " in both the Matthæan and Lucan versions of the Paternoster. "Give us this day our *epiousios* bread." What did *epiousios* mean? It did not occur anywhere else in the New Testament. Careful search for an instance of its use was made through all existing Greek literature, but in vain. Through century after century the problem remained unsolved. Even the great scholar Origen, who was born so far back as A.D. 185 and heard in everyday use the same kind of Greek as that in which the New Testament is written, had to confess that he did not know the word, and had failed to discover anyone who could tell him. "It seems likely," he adds, "that it was moulded by the Evangelists"— that they invented it for use in this special place. When St. Jerome made his Latin translation of the Bible, which was finished about A.D. 400, he guessed that the meaning of *epiousios* might be "daily". From the Latin of the Vulgate the word "daily" got into the Lord's Prayer of our Prayerbook.

But suppose in our reading we came across an English word which was unknown to us, and could not be found in any dictionary. In order to discover its meaning, we should naturally ask ourselves what other word or words it resembled, from one of which it might be derived? To illustrate the point, let us invent an imaginary word, "resignment", and suppose we had met it in a book. Having consulted the dictionary in vain, we should try to get a clue to its meaning by asking what other word it resembled. And the obvious answer would be that "resignment" must be connected with the verb "to resign." Then, however, another question, less easy to answer, might suggest itself. Was the new word connected with "to resign", to give up, or with "to re-sign", to sign again? That is, more or less, the kind of problem which confronted scholars as they examined the word *epiousios*. Three possible derivations were in turn suggested. According to the first, the adjective, taken together with "bread", would mean "bread for our subsistence". According to the second, it would mean "bread for the present

74

time ". But there were serious philological objections to both these explanations. The third interpretation made the phrase signify " bread for the soon-coming time " ; i.e. " bread for the morrow ". For some time past virtually all scholars have accepted this third derivation.

Then, within recent years, the skilful examination of ancient papyri recovered from the sands of Egypt has opened a new chapter in the history of New Testament research, a chapter of which even more important pages may remain to be written in the near future. Already the discoveries have included copies of large parts of the New Testament at least a century older than the Codex Sinaiticus. Again, many thousands of domestic and business writings have been found, some of them complete, others but small fragments—letters, contracts, household lists, all manner of things. These were written in the same kind of Greek as the New Testament books, and their practical value is in the light they throw upon the meaning of many words which previously were thought to occur only in those

books. And in a papyrus the word
epiousios at last was found, proving that
Origen was mistaken in his idea that the
Evangelists invented it. "This word
has been established beyond doubt by
the new study ", wrote the late Professor
Deissmann, one of the greatest authorities
on the subject. He described the papyrus
as " the remains of a housekeeper's book."
And, turning to the use of the word in
the Paternoster, he added : " The strict
meaning of the prayer is : Give us
to-day our amount of daily food for
to-morrow."* Dr. Moffatt's rendering
of St. Matthew vi, 11, is : " Give us
to-day our bread for the morrow."

II

We will assume, then, this to be the
true meaning. Before noticing in detail
how real is the gain which it brings, let
us remark that there is no corresponding

* " The New Testament in the Light of Modern
Research ": the Haskell Lectures, 1929, By Adolf
Deissmann, pp. 84, 86.

loss ; that the force of the petition as
we have used it hitherto still remains.
The main thought, doubtless, which the
words " Give us this day our daily bread "
suggested was that we look to God for
the things (in the Prayer-book phrase)
" requisite and necessary as well for the
body as the soul " ; that our bodily needs
are not forgotten by our Father, and
that we have Christ's authority for praying about them. The new rendering still
leaves us the welcome comfort of that
truth. As much as ever our sense of
dependence on God is emphasized. Yet
the precise point of emphasis is changed.
The old thought, though retained in its
fullness, becomes subsidiary to the new.
In their main significance the words are
now less a prayer for food than a prayer
for peace of mind. The reason of our
asking for the food is that we may be
freed from anxiety. " Give us—not
accumulated wealth, nor heaped-up stores
for all the days to come—we do not ask
that—but give us sufficient simple
provender in hand that our lives may not
be marred by over-anxiety about the

morrow. Give us to-day to-morrow's bread."

Let us think of the people to whom first our Lord taught this prayer—the people amongst whom He lived and worked. A few of them were rich. A few were so poor as to be destitute. But the most of them were, as we should say, people of narrow means. So long as they could earn their wages they managed well enough. Only there was nothing to spare. They had no margin. The day's wage had to buy the day's food. If an unexpected guest arrived, there would be nothing in the cupboard; the host must try to borrow some provision from a neighbour. With people so circumstanced, one of the worst troubles, affecting their whole thought and making them less easily reached by any spiritual message, was this uncertainty about the necessaries of life, this so frequent worry about to-morrow's food. The Gospels show that our Lord found it a real obstacle to His mission. It engrossed the hearts of men, making them slow to receive His message. It precluded that

78

serene tranquillity of mind which was
His own, which He longed to impart to
His followers. They were apt to be
absorbed by the task of obtaining " the
meat which perisheth," by their material
wants. Our Lord tried to combat this
influence. He spoke about it explicitly,
urging His listeners to master over-
anxiety about the morrow, this worry
over obtaining food and drink and clothes.
But He gave them His sympathy too,
for He Himself had known want, and
had felt the downward pull of material
needs. He understood how hard it was
for them to heed spiritual teaching unless
they could be liberated from this worry,
by knowing that they had something in
hand. So He encouraged them to pray
for it, and to ask that God would remove
their need for anxiety by letting them
possess enough for the morrow. " Give
us to-day," they were to pray, " to-
morrow's bread."

III

If this be the true meaning of the
sentence, it is not one we shall value
lightly. In the first of the petitions we
are taught to make for ourselves, we
ask to be made, not wealthy, but sure of
the morrow, exempt from the mental
troubles which militate fiercely against
the life of the soul. And the presence
of this clause in the Lord's Prayer shows
that He sympathizes with us about this.
He knows the evil influence of worry,
on soul and body alike. Worry kills more
people in this country each year than does
influenza or any other plague.

Experience confirms, too, the understanding wisdom shown in the wording
of the sentence. It is not so much the
present difficulty that is hard to bear
as the less definite troubles about the
future, the absence of a margin, the fears
about to-morrow's bread. Probably this
trial was never more common than in
our own age, with its financial stringency
and unsettled outlook. We find it in

many walks of life. Here—to take instances almost at random—is a working-man ; he has a job at the moment, but is afraid of being turned adrift to-morrow. Here is a journalist who has served his paper through long years. He has given it his best. But there are rumours of a changed proprietorship and many dis-missals ; his heart is sick with fear about to-morrow's bread. Here is a clerk, on an income which makes saving impossible. The office talk is of economies and a reduced staff. What, he wonders, is to become then of his delicate wife and children ? Or the writer with a dwindling market, or a minor actress near the end of a run, or the elderly governess, or the professional worker with increasing expenses and diminishing income. . . .

Were it an actually present trouble, of which they knew the worst, it would be easier to bear, than this harassing un-certainty about the future. They live their lives bravely, they try to hope for the best ; few of their friends and none of their acquaintances are allowed to guess that they are haunted by this

81

F

spectre of anxiety. Yet there are solitary moments in the dark of night when the burden seems almost greater than they can bear. Had they only, as we say, something to fall back upon, had they some little store in hand, their whole prospect would be transformed.

IV

I need not multiply examples. Do we not all know, in some degree, these fears about our future, or about the futures of those we love? And, when it becomes acute, this anxiety preys not only upon physical but upon spiritual health. It becomes extraordinarily difficult for people to lift their thoughts to the highest things while they are obsessed by these haunting worries, and have nothing in hand. It is this that they crave—to have some security, to feel that, whatever to-morrow's need, they have provision for it safe in store. "Give us to-day," they ask, "to-morrow's bread!" It seems a thought to be treasured that when

we use this sentence of the Lord's Prayer
we are praying for all these people, the
anxious and heavy laden; all the brave
folk who carry on stoutly, yet at heart are
dismayed by the fear of a breadless
morrow—dismayed, likely enough, far
less for themselves than for the sake of
wife, or husband, or children. As we
understood the words in the past, we
prayed in this clause of the Paternoster for
bodily needs alone. " Give us the bread
we need to-day." As this other rendering
interprets it, we pray for tranquillity of
mind as well as for bodily food; in fact,
our reason for asking that we may have
the necessaries of bodily life in advance
is that thereby we may secure peace of
mind. And we ask for peace of mind
because a disquieted mind wars against
the life of the soul.

When we think again of the humble
folk to whom first our Lord gave His
Prayer, we can understand how readily
they would welcome and use the sentence
which prayed to-day for to-morrow's
bread. The question has been asked,
however, whether to use the petition

in this sense is consistent with our Lord's exhortation to " take no thought for the morrow." Yet the answer is simple. The command was not really to take no thought for the morrow, but as the Revised version rightly indicates, " be not anxious," " be not over anxious," " do not worry " about to-morrow. And then in the Lord's Prayer He bids us pray for what will remove the cause of over-anxiety. Indeed, the best safe-guard against it is to cast our cares upon God, to bring our wants for the morrow before Him in prayer.

And the prayer is heard. In ways past finding out, in ways past man's under-standing, God does supply the needs of those who trust Him. Theirs (the history of a myriad disciples confirms the fact) is a tranquillity of mind which has grown out of experience. For each coming day God makes provision before-hand, until the last—and beyond the last. He will give us to-day, in this sense also, to-morrow's bread ; will bestow now the strength we shall need when this day is done. To the life spent apart from God the evening comes chill and disconsolate : the shadows thicken as the end seems near. To the life with God also evening comes—yet it is no ending of life. Faith feels the night-wind, and knows it for the herald of fresh youth. Faith views the tranquil sundown, and sees in its last glow a promise of the leaping dawn.

VI

FORGIVENESS

I

THERE are some slight but interesting differences of wording in the petition for forgiveness as recorded in the First and Third Gospels. St. Matthew's version, literally rendered, is :

> Forgive us our debts,
> As we also have forgiven our debtors ;

and St. Luke's :

> Forgive us our sins,
> For we also ourselves forgive every one that is indebted to us.

Another interesting variant is that of the Old Syriac version, which seems often to reproduce the original Aramaic with special fidelity. In place of the Matthæan "we have forgiven," or the Lucan "we forgive," it has "we will forgive."

According to the First Gospel, those using the Prayer say that they have forgiven already ; according to the Third, that they forgive habitually ; in the Syriac version they promise that they will forgive. With all, obviously, the sense is practically identical ; in each he who uses the Prayer accepts the condition, on which our Lord insisted often, that we may not ask forgiveness of God unless we ourselves are ready to forgive our fellow-men. Such slight variations may represent, as we have seen already, slightly differing forms of the Prayer as taught by our Lord at different times. But the Matthæan " debts " seems more probably the equivalent of what He said than the Lucan " sins." This evangelist himself has " debtors " in the second half of the sentence, and we may feel sure that the thought of the two parts—" our debts," " our debtors," would correspond. " Forgiveness of sins " was a phrase so constantly used in New Testament and other early Christian writings that we can easily understand how it would come naturally to mind and be written down in place of

forgiveness of " debts." Yet our con-
viction that " debts," used by St.
Matthew, more probably represents the
word used by our Lord Himself in teaching the Prayer is strengthened when we
recollect other passages in which he
enforced the same truth. Particularly we
shall remember the parable of the Two
Debtors—of the man who was forgiven
a debt of pounds but would not forgive
a debt of pence.

Again, it may be thought that the
difference of meaning between " sins "
and " debts " is not important. The Greek
word rendered " sins " means literally " a
missing of the mark," so that " going
astray " or " trespass " represents it
accurately. The word rendered " debt "
means, when not used figuratively, a
literal " money-debt," and has been found
in this sense in various papyri. It is
true, of course, that all " sin " is, in some
degree, a failure to pay our just debts to
God—our debt of obedience, our debt
of gratitude. Yet I incline to think that
there is a distinction, and that when
Jesus bade us pray " forgive us our

88

debts " His choice of this word shows Him to have meant particularly what are termed " faults of omission." These, in the strict sense, are debts to God which we have failed to pay.

It was upon these that He laid most stress in His doctrine. To regain its force, we must needs remember how amazingly novel it seemed to the people of His time. His standards and values differed widely from those of their accredited religious teachers. They, it is true, described " righteousness " as man's supreme aim, and the casual listener might hear this new Rabbi also extolling " righteousness," and therefore following apparently, the accustomed lines. But as he heard more, he discovered " with increasing astonishment " (such is the precise meaning of the word used by the Evangelists) that the content of our Lord's teaching, the ideas he held about the nature of " righteousness," were wholly new. In particular—this is the point which concerns us here—He seemed to be grieved by what men abstained from doing rather than by what they did.

With us it has become a truism that
His positive teaching contrasted with the
Rabbi's negative morality, that His
" thou shalt " replaced the old " thou
shalt not." Yet even now it may be
doubted if we have made our moral code
approximate to that of Jesus, or really
have adopted His scale of values, His
categories of right and wrong. He made
astonishingly little of what were reckoned
serious offences; the omissions, the
failures to use opportunities of doing
good were the faults He condemned
unsparingly. He put before His hearers
a tremendous picture of a final judgment;
its setting was reproduced, to a great
extent, from Apocalyptic writings, but its
appraisals of conduct were emphatically
new. And in that picture, as we shall
remember, the hapless condemned " at
the left hand " were not they who, in the
common phrase, " had done wrong," but
they who had failed to do right—they
who wilfully had missed opportunities
for kindness, for comforting, for helping,
for shewing love to their neighbours.

Therefore it is strictly consonant with

the rest of His teaching that His prayer
bids us ask that we may be forgiven less
for the wrong things we have done, than
for the right things we have failed to do ;
not "forgive us our trespasses," but
"forgive us our debts." Our trespasses
also need forgiveness, beyond doubt.
Yet He might suppose that, without
prompting, we should seek God's pardon
for these, while we are apt to think of
less account, or to ignore entirely, those
faults of omission which in fact are
more serious. Many a conscience is not
seriously perturbed as it reviews the
definitely wrong actions of which it has
cognizance. Without undue boasting, a
great many people are able to feel that
—if only through the circumstances of
their lives, their upbringing, and their
freedom from the grosser temptations—
they have been able to keep themselves
comparatively innocent of what are com-
monly regarded as heinous sins. Their
lapses (for which they are quite ready
to ask the Divine forgiveness) have
not been, they feel, very numerous. On
the whole, they do not seem to them-

selves to have done a great deal of wrong. But how this complacency crumbles away if they come to apprehend Christ's view, and reckon the loss of each opportunity for doing good as real sin ! How innumerable are the debts to God and our neighbour—and to God through our neighbour—we have failed to pay ! Yet it is these—these lost opportunities, it seems—which Jesus thought the most serious of all failings. Does not that truth drive home to us our need of forgiveness ?

Therefore, if we retain the familiar form of words and say " Forgive us our trespasses " when we repeat the Paternoster we shall not use the sentence rightly unless we remember its true meaning, given in the Bible version of the Prayer, " forgive us our debts "— remission of debts left unpaid, forgiveness for missed opportunities, for kind words and deeds unsaid and undone. " Forgive us our debts ! "

II

To remember this meaning will add also to the poignancy which the second clause of the petition has for us. In practice it is the " debts " owed to us but unpaid, that we find hardest to forgive our neighbour. No doubt, if we think that he has done us a definite wrong by word or deed, the task of forgiving him from our hearts is none too easy. Yet easier it is than to forgive those who have made no effort to pay what we had every right to expect. Perhaps we have done much for them. We have a substantial claim on their gratitude. But when in turn we need their help, when a little kindness or sympathy from them would mean much, and we, who have relied upon it, find that it is withheld—then the sense of injury rankles, and we do not find it easy to forgive these debtors of ours. " As we also have forgiven our debtors " is probably a more difficult word to say with full sincerity than " as we forgive them that trespass against

93

us." Yet it has to be said, if we are to
ask that our own debts to God be
remitted.

If we wonder why Jesus seemed to
view as so far more serious the faults of
omission than those of commission, the
reason does not seem beyond our understanding. We may remember that many
of the deeds condemned by popular
opinion as the worst sins were offences,
in part, against a real moral law, but in
part also merely against a sociological
code, with a basis human rather than
divine. To neglect a chance of kindness
on the contrary, was, in the view of
Christ, to sin against the law of love—
far more important, in His view, than
any other. Again, we shall be helped
to understand His judgment when we
remember the view of God bestowed by
Him, and emphasized in the first words
of this Prayer. It is addressed to " our
Father." There is no fault of children
which pains a father so deeply as ingratitude. Let us imagine the instance of
two sons ; one of them gets into some
foolish entanglement, or runs up bills

extravagantly. He has done wrong, yet
him the father, remembering the temptations of his own hot youth, will find it
not very difficult to forgive. The other
is a pattern of outward decorum. But he
is self-centred and selfish. His father,
being unwell, hopes that his son will
keep him company for a few days. He
does not suggest it, longing that the son
should propose it himself. But the son
departs, having a more attractive engage-
ment elsewhere. He gives never a thought
to all that the father has done for him,
the self-sacrifice which provided a good
education; he makes no attempt at all
to repay even a little of this debt of
kindness. He ignores it with bland
complacency. Will not the father find
this attitude much harder to forgive than
the other son's lapses from virtue, be
grieved far more by the one's faults of
omission than by the other's faults of
commission? And as God's relation with
us (so Jesus taught) is that of a loving
father with his children, do we not get
a glimpse of the manner in which He
must sorrow over our terrible lack of

gratitude, our so frequent forgetfulness of all we owe to him? Thinking of this, we seem to understand why our Lord has taught us in His Prayer to say, "Forgive us our debts."

Perhaps a word should be added about the second part of the sentence. When we pray "Forgive us . . . as we forgive," clearly that does not mean a request that the Divine forgiveness shall be merely proportionate to ours. Ill would it be for us were there, so to speak, an exact scale of reciprocity, if the pardon we may hope to receive could not exceed the pardon we were able to bestow. We know that our unpaid debts to God are vastly greater than any owed to us by our fellow-men. St. Luke's version of the Prayer safeguards us against such misunderstanding. It replaces "as" by "for," so that unmistakably the petition is not "forgive us *in proportion as* we forgive," but "forgive us *because* we forgive." When we use the words, we affirm that we are trying to fulfil the condition which justifies us in asking forgiveness. We may try imperfectly, yet at least we try. Before we can make the petition for ourselves, we must try to let the spirit of charity and forgiveness take possession of our hearts. So shall we put ourselves in tune with God, and be made ready to ask, without unfitness, for His pardon. Then, indeed, we are certain of gaining it. For the actions of God, as Jesus taught, are not arbitrary and capricious. They are controlled immutably by His own law. Accordingly, it is no mere matter of speculation whether or no God remits our debts. Two conditions must be fulfilled. There must be real "repentance" for our failures—which means no mere emotional regret but a steadfast purpose to do better. And there must be the spirit of forgiveness towards our debtors. Let these two things be present, and we can ask forgiveness in full certainty that the prayer will be answered. So prayed, it must gain its end, by God's perpetual law.

G

III

An attempt to study in full our Lord's teaching about forgiveness would take us too far from our present theme. Yet to understand and use rightly these words of the Paternoster will set us free from misunderstandings that are strangely common. People still speak as though the Master had enjoined a forgiveness quite indiscriminate. His words show how false an idea is this. For one thing we are to be ready to forgive the wrong-doer whenever he shall show penitence, but not before; " if thy brother sin against thee and he repent, forgive him," is the command; if our forgiveness is to be moulded upon God's, then we know that to forgive while there was exultant persistence in wrong-doing would be no act of true love. And, for another thing, it is not wrongs in general, still less wrongs done to others, but wrongs done to ourselves only, which we are to be ready to forgive. Not—reverting for a moment to the familiar rendering of

the Prayer—" as we forgive them that
trespass," but strictly " them that trespass
against us." Other injuries must be left
to another judgment. Only when we
ourselves have suffered have we ourselves
the duty and honour of forgiving. Such
is the spirit, then, in which we shall make
this petition ; mindful of our illimitable
failures, our ingratitude, our swiftness
to judge others harshly. " Forgive us
our debts. And this we ask, resolved
ourselves to forgive our debtors."

VII

TEMPTATION AND EVIL

I

"Not into temptation." . . . Concerning these words much has been written, for the sentence in which they stand has generally been accounted the most difficult of the Lord's Prayer. But the point of difficulty has shifted within modern times, so that of the newer problem there seems to be still something which needs to be said. True, neither the child at a mother's knee nor the aged cottager repeating the Prayer will stray far from the essential meaning. Each, at least, knows temptation; each asks to be delivered from evil. Rightly, however, we desire more than a general idea of the significance which the sentence possesses. The more closely we examine the Paternoster, the more spiritually vital it becomes; the more our eyes are

opened to the wealth of teaching beneath
the simplicity of phrase. And it is, I
believe, by a close scrutiny of the exact
wording that we may hope to solve the
problems and arrive at the true force of
this final petition in the Lord's Prayer.

Of the older and more familiar difficulty
little, perhaps, need be said now, but it
seems to have been felt keenly in the
earlier days of the Christian Church.
" Are we to believe," men asked, " that
God leads us into temptation ? If so,

O Thou, who didst with pitfall and with gin
Beset the Road I was to wander in,
    Thou wilt not with Predestin'd Evil round
Enmesh, and then impute my Fall to Sin ! "

We shrink from such a thought—yet
how else is it needful, as Jesus teaches, to
beseech the Father that He will not lead
us into temptation ? From very early
times some people had tried to excuse
their misdeeds by assigning the blame to
God, and the author of Ecclesiasticus
reproved them : " Say not thou : It is
through the Lord that I fell away. . . .
Say not thou : It is He that caused me to

err." Afterwards St. James repeated the warning, in his own blunt fashion : " Let no man say when he is tempted : I am tempted of God." Was he driven to enforce this because already the sentence of the paternoster had been misunderstood, and mischievous arguments were based on the misunderstanding ? In later years we may be sure that the difficulty was increased through the rendering of the Greek phrase by "ne nos *inducas*" in Latin, and, from the Latin, by "*Lead* us not" in English. Those words would be the right equivalent of another Greek verb than that which is used ; in the one actually employed there is no such strong directive sense. The Revised Version has recognized this by putting "Bring us not" in place of "Lead us not," and we might wish that "Bring us not" were adopted in our liturgical use of the Prayer. Yet that change, though it would lessen, would not remove the difficulty—the difficulty of supposing the words to imply that God, unless our prayers intervened, might bring man into temptation.

The way to the right understanding of them seems to be shown by some variants of the sentence which were both very ancient and very widespread. Indeed, these " glosses " often passed from liturgical versions of the Prayer, where, in all probability, they originated, into actual texts of the Matthæan and Lucan Gospels. The most felicitous, perhaps, is that quoted by St. Augustine : " Many people when using the Prayer word this sentence ' Suffer us not to be led into temptation.' " (*Multi precando ita dicunt : Ne nos patiaris induci in tentationem.*) This turn of the sentence, given it in very early times, persisted through centuries, and passed, indeed, into our own tongue. Among its champions was Henry VIII. When the " Bishops' Book " was to be rewritten and reissued as the " Necessary Learning " of 1543, Henry sent Cranmer a copy of the earlier work in which he had noted the very numerous alterations he desired. Among them, he wished the sentence in the Paternoster to read : " And let us not be led into temptation ". Cranmer demurred. " Christ taught us thus to

that ever lived could be exempt from it.
Nor for our Lord Himself in His earthly
life was this possible. And we are not
to suppose that his only temptations were
those he faced in solitude immediately
after the Baptism. There were others
which beset Him throughout His ministry,
and some at least—perhaps the temptation
to abandon His work in the face of
hostility and seeming failure—He bore in
common with His disciples. " Ye are
they," He said to them near the end,
" which have continued with me in my
temptations." How, then, can we ask
to be spared that which is, in fact, inevitable ? Why should we seem to ask for
escape from the common lot of human
nature ? What do we really mean when
we say, " Lead us not into temptation ? "

A commentator of the older school
cites the words as an example of our
Lord's " idealism." We are told that
" as He commanded His disciples to be
perfect, though knowing well that perfection far exceeded their reach, so here He
bids them pray for the ideal state, for
freedom from all temptation, although

in this world the prayer cannot be completely answered." The reader will agree, I think, that this is a most unsatisfying explanation. It is one thing to propound an ideal standard of human conduct; it is quite another to implore God daily to grant what, in point of fact, we know He cannot grant. Moreover—and here we touch the heart of the difficulty—" freedom from temptation " would *not* be " the ideal state " for human beings in this world. To desire it would be, speaking bluntly, the height of foolishness, would be to ignore all that God has revealed concerning moral growth.

For we have learnt no longer to confuse temptation with sin. We see that the potential good of temptation is as real as its potential evil. We understand how fundamental is the law of effort as the condition of all progress. Science has taught us to discern its operation in the physical world, and to see struggle crowned by survival in the cosmic evolutionary process. And in the spiritual world also it is he who overcometh that spiritual sloth by being brought into special temptation and so falling into sin." That is an explanation which needs explanation. It seems to imply that the Divine method of remedying our spiritual sloth is to cause us to fall into sin. But, apart from any such special point, this is one of the many explanations which are far too subtle and intricate. They seem to forget that the Prayer was given originally for use by the simple peasant and fisher folk of Galilee. Surely it is incredible that, among the very concise, lucid, and definite petitions of His model Prayer, our Lord should have introduced one that could be understood only if its words were construed in an abnormal sense, one that could be made intelligible only by an elaborate and arbitrary paraphrase.

Yet it seems equally impossible to disregard the precise wording, as Bishop Gore proposed, and " to interpret the prayer more generally as an expression of self-distrust." That, no doubt, it is. Yet it cannot be merely to express our self-distrust that we are bidden to pray

"Bring us not into temptation," especially when we remember that only by meeting temptation can we gain strength. Would our Lord wish our self-distrust to be expressed by asking that we should miss the one experience which makes spiritual growth possible? No; the explanation of these simple and direct words must itself be direct and simple. It must lie within the words themselves, not in dubious inferences which may be drawn from them. And such an explanation seems ready to our hand.

III

The petition is that we may not be brought *into* temptation. That is quite different from a petition that we may not be brought *unto* temptation. As if to stress the point, the preposition is duplicated in Greek, in a way that cannot be reproduced in English; "do not into- bring us into temptation" would be its literal equivalent. And, as a standard

us from evil" merely completes and illuminates the prayer "bring us not into temptation." The Greek words at the close may mean either "from evil" or "from the evil one"; on the whole, I think the impersonal rendering, as we have it in the familiar English version of the Prayer, gives us better sense. The point is, however, not of great importance. But we ought to notice carefully the preceding words. Those translated "deliver us" mean literally "draw us away to Thyself," and the preposition is "from," not "out of" evil. Therefore the force of the whole cannot be, as some have supposed, "Suffer us, so far as possible, not to be led into temptation; but when, through our inevitable frailty, we have been led into it, help us to escape again out of its evil." Rather we ask that, when brought to temptation, we may not be brought into it, but may be saved from that entrance by the power of God, drawing us back from the evil to Himself.

Let us use a prosaic illustration to make the point clear. A man whose special weakness is drink has daily to pass a public-

important points. It seems as much in place in some distant mission station—where, probably, it is the first written word to be translated—as in St. Paul's in London, or in St. Peter's at Rome. It can be lisped with understanding by a young child. It astonishes the wisest by its profundity. Its larger—the Matthæan—form consists, in Greek, of fifty-seven words. What is there that we can desire to ask, what need is there of human life, which these astoundingly few sentences fail to express? Yes, the more we ponder and use these words, the surer we grow concerning Him Who spake them.

How comforting, therefore, is their revelation of the mind of God! This Prayer shows that He understands and feels with us in our needs and difficulties. In it there is no suggestion of Divine anger caused by our distrust, our failures, our weakness in face of temptation. But there is encouragement to tell God of these things, and to ask His help. And the fact that He bids us ask seems a pledge that the Prayer will be answered. There are times when we grow impatient